PAMPHLETS ON AMERICAN WRITERS · NUMBER 2

UNIVERSITY OF MINNESOTA

⟍ *Robert Frost*

BY LAWRANCE THOMPSON

UNIVERSITY OF MINNESOTA PRESS · MINNEAPOLIS

⌐ Foreword

AMERICAN literature is one of the world's youngest literatures. In many ways it is an offshoot of English literature, but, as the editor of the London *Times Literary Supplement* said a few years ago, it has achieved its own independence and vigor. Especially in the years since World War II, both in the United States and in other countries, the interest in American writers has increased greatly.

The University of Minnesota Pamphlets on American Writers are designed to help satisfy this interest. The editors and advisers hope that students in various parts of the world will bring to these pamphlets the same sort of attention that serious students, in either hemisphere or in whatever zone, have traditionally brought to the various national literatures that have engaged their minds and have stimulated their imaginations. They also hope each pamphlet will provide a worthwhile critical summary (as well as a brief biographical sketch and bibliography) that will serve the needs of mature readers in all countries. Ideally, of course, each pamphlet should send the reader to the writer's own books, upon which he can pass his own critical judgments.

In the seventeenth and eighteenth centuries the United States produced only a small number of writers. In the nineteenth century the number increased greatly, and in the twentieth it has become almost a flood. In the opinion of the editors and advisers the authors being discussed in this series are those who have won, or seem to deserve, a place among the world's important writers.

William Van O'Connor, Allen Tate, and
Robert Penn Warren, EDITORS

ROBERT FROST

LAWRANCE THOMPSON is a professor of English and American literature at Princeton University. He is the author of several books of literary criticism including *Fire and Ice: The Art and Thought of Robert Frost,* and he is preparing a biography of Robert Frost.

⌁ *Robert Frost*

I~N~ Robert Frost's dramatic dialogue entitled "West-running Brook" a farmer and his wife are represented as admiring the contrary direction of a small New England stream which must turn eastward, somewhere, to flow into the Atlantic. As they talk, they notice how the black water, catching on a sunken rock, flings a white wave backward, against the current. The husband says,

> "Speaking of contraries, see how the brook
> In that white wave runs counter to itself."

Within the poem, various "contraries" are interlocked to illuminate one of the poet's major and recurrent themes; yet no harm is done the poem if that wave image is borrowed, temporarily, for use in another sense. It can serve to suggest a possible approach to an interpretation of Robert Frost's life and art, in terms of elements which there run counter to themselves.

Start with a few "contraries" implicit in the story of his life. Widely celebrated as a New England poet, Robert Frost was actually born in San Francisco, California, on March 26, 1874. Although his father was a native of New England, his mother was a true Scots woman, an emigrant from Edinburgh. She had been well educated in Columbus, Ohio, had become a schoolteacher, and had met her future husband while both of them were teaching school in Lewistown, Pennsylvania. Because Isabelle Moodie Frost was fond of writing verse, it would not have been surprising if she had named her son after Robert Burns; but as it happened the father chose to name the child after the South's most distinguished general, Robert E. Lee.

Further contraries are suggested by the motives for that naming.

The poet's father, William Prescott Frost, was descended from a puritanic line of Maine and New Hampshire farmers, public servants, and Revolutionary War soldiers. Yet William had developed such a violent hatred for his native New England that he had remained only long enough to be graduated with honors from Harvard College, in the class of 1872. Thereupon he had started west, pausing for one year of teaching at Lewistown to acquire funds, and then, with his new wife at his side, moving on to seek his fortune in the Golden Gate city. Part of his hatred for New England had been engendered by the Civil War, which had interrupted the flow of raw cotton from the South to factories in New England. William's father, having abandoned farming in his native New Hampshire in order to try his luck as a worker in the cotton and woolen mills along the Merrimack River at Lawrence, Massachusetts, had become a foreman in one of those mills. But when local economies were upset by the Civil War and by the shortage of raw cotton, he and many other New Englanders had found their sympathies thus bound up with the southern cause.

Raised as a city boy, in San Francisco, until he was eleven years old, Robert Lee Frost found his life uprooted when his father died there of tuberculosis, in 1885, leaving as his only will the seemingly inconsistent request that his remains be taken back to his native and hated New England for burial. Thus it happened that the boy crossed the continent with his mother and his younger sister, Jeanie. Because funds were not available for the return trip to California, the widow and her children settled in the village of Salem, New Hampshire, where Mrs. Frost earned a precarious living for a few years, teaching in the grammar school which her children attended.

Robert Frost has often said that when first he came to New England he prided himself so much on being a Californian that he felt a decided hostility toward those reticent Yankees whose

4

idiom he later honored in his poetry. Perhaps it was the shock of newness which sharpened his various responses to those peculiar New England speech-ways, images, scenes, characters, and attitudes.

Disliking study, and refusing to read any book by himself until he was twelve, the boy suddenly developed an intense pleasure in learning, during his four years in the Lawrence High School. After he was graduated as valedictorian, and class poet, in 1892, he enrolled as a freshman at Dartmouth College, but soon left, insisting that he had had enough of scholarship. During the next few years, seemingly without any worldly ambition, he tried his hand at various ways of earning a living. At different times, he worked in mills in Lawrence, dabbled in newspaper reporting, taught school. Meanwhile, his fondness for writing poetry occupied his leisure hours. In 1894, to celebrate his first sale of a poem, "My Butterfly," to a prominent literary magazine, the *New York Independent*, he arranged to have six of his lyrics privately printed in a booklet entitled *Twilight*. The edition was limited to only two copies, one for his affianced, Elinor White, and one for himself.

After his marriage in 1895, he tried to settle into the routine of schoolteaching. For more than two years he helped his mother manage a small private school in Lawrence, then spent two years as a special student at Harvard College, hoping to prepare himself for college teaching. But again he decided that the academic atmosphere was not congenial to him. On an impulse, he tried to make a successful business enterprise out of raising hens and selling eggs. In 1900, when a doctor warned him that his recurrent illnesses (largely nervous) might indicate tuberculosis, he moved with his growing family to a small farm in Derry, New Hampshire, and there continued his poultry business.

Nothing went well for him, and he seemed to have a gift for

failure only. During the winter of 1906, he came so near to death, from pneumonia, that both he and his doctor were surprised when he recovered. Thus reduced to the verge of nothingness, and feeling completely without prospects, he turned more and more to his almost furtive writing of poetry, as a kind of consolation. Occasionally he sold a poem or two. But when he was forced to admit that he could not make ends meet, financially, as either poet or farmer, he turned again to schoolteaching, this time at Pinkerton Academy in Derry. Subsequently, he taught psychology for one year at the New Hampshire State Normal School in Plymouth.

Having grown accustomed to gambling with his own life, he decided, in 1912, to bet all on poetry. After selling his farm in Derry, Frost took his wife and four children to England, rented a house in Beaconsfield, Buckinghamshire, and settled in, to write. The gamble was very successful. Much to his relief, his first book of lyrics, *A Boy's Will* (1913), was accepted by the first publisher to whom it was offered. His book of dramatic dialogues, *North of Boston* (1914), attracted so much attention that by the time the Frost family returned to the United States, early in 1915, both books had been reissued there, and *North of Boston* was on its way to becoming a best seller.

Success embarrassed him. Extremely shy, painfully sensitive, inwardly tortured by crowds, Frost bought a small farm in Franconia, New Hampshire, hoping to escape from public adulation. For reasons of economics and pride, however, he could not long refuse invitations to give public lectures and readings. In less than a year after his return from England he had publicly performed in various parts of the United States, literally from Maine to Texas. Then in spite of his asserted distaste for all things academic, he became one of the first American poets to make arrangements with various institutions to live on campus as poet-

in-residence, for a few months or years. While his major relationships of this sort were with Amherst College in Massachusetts,
he has also spent intermittent years in residence at the University
of Michigan, at Harvard College, and at Dartmouth.

Throughout these various sojourns as troubadour, Frost has
managed to indulge his liking for the life of a farmer, particularly during vacation months of seedtime, growth, and harvest.
He left New Hampshire for Vermont when he moved with his
family from Franconia to South Shaftsbury and bought a farm
there in 1919. After his children had grown, and after Mrs. Frost
had died, he changed his legal residence from South Shaftsbury
to an upland farm which he purchased in Ripton, Vermont. On
doctor's orders he began spending the most severe winter months
in Florida, starting in 1936; then in 1940 he bought a rural acre
outside Coral Gables, Florida, and built a typical New England
bungalow on that semitropical farm. His feeling for the soil and
for growing things remained a passion with him, long after that
kind of life ceased to be a necessity.

Having survived without any public recognition until his for-
tieth year, Frost thereafter received more honors than any other
contemporary literary figure in America. He was elected to membership in the National Institute of Arts and Letters in 1916, to
membership in the American Academy in 1930. Four times he
has been awarded the Pulitzer Prize for Poetry. On the occasion
of his seventy-fifth birthday, and again on his eighty-fifth, the
United States Senate adopted a formal resolution extending felici-
tations to him. In spite of his resistance to earning even the
lowliest college diploma, he has been given honorary degrees by
more than forty colleges and universities. One phase of his career
came full circle in the spring of 1957, when he returned to England (where he had gone as a complete stranger in 1912) to
receive honorary degrees from Oxford and Cambridge.

7

Further patterns of contraries can be found within and between the arrangements of Robert Frost's ten separate volumes
of poems. In the lyrics of *A Boy's Will*, representing the long
long thoughts of the artist as a young man, the stanzaic forms
follow the conventions of the couplet, the quatrain, the sonnet,
and the ballad. Certain archaisms reflect his indebtedness to
earlier poets. But even in those earliest poems, Frost's idiom is
revealed in a clearly established willingness to displace the nine-
teenth-century tradition of musical sounds by emphasizing dramatic intonations and cadences of everyday conversational speech,
in a simple vocabulary, and with typical Yankee understatement.

The consciously arranged pattern of lyrics in *A Boy's Will* is
designed to represent the poet's youthful growth in a wavering
progression of subjective moods. Independent searchings, ques-
tionings, doubtings, affirmings, cherishings, are dramatically and
poetically realized at times with an implied disregard for conventional attitudes; but at other times these lyrics constitute
rediscoveries which frankly refresh the truths of the common-
place. The gestures of quest begin with the poet's acknowledged
need for separateness and isolation ("Into My Own"), progress
through a subtly intense group of love-and-courtship lyrics
("Love and a Question," "A Late Walk," "Flower-Gathering,"
"A Dream Pang"), turn to a newly perceived sense of the brother-
hood of men "whether they work together or apart" ("A Tuft of
Flowers"), and finally circle back to a mood of isolation which
has become wistful ("Reluctance").

That circular or rather spiral pattern of complementary moods,
in *A Boy's Will*, is enriched by an arranged progression of responses to the seasonal cycle of nature, starting with a subdued
enjoyment of the autumnal mood, moving through deeds and
images of winter, spring, summer, and finally returning "with a
difference" to autumnal settings. In these variations of attitudes

toward nature, the young and maturing poet's moods entertain different values at different times. If at one moment nature seems to him indifferent and blind toward man's "faltering few steps" between birth and death (as in "Stars"), and momentarily malevolent, hostile, bestial (as in "Storm Fear"), it can also at times reflect a benevolently divine plan or design (as in "A Prayer in Spring"). These various contradictions of mood are permitted to remain unresolved within the formal structural arrangement of the lyrics, a pattern which establishes a sort of matrix for later poetic insights and outlooks.

By contrast, *North of Boston* is "a book of people," wherein the prevailing mode is dramatic narrative and dramatic dialogue. The poet's attention is directed outward, rather than inward, as he portrays a variety of rural New England responses to the human predicament, not for purposes of recording "local color" but rather to evoke universal extensions of meaning. The kinship of these poems with the idylls of Theocritus is not accidental. Predominantly, these blank-verse narratives of rural manners and ways focus attention on psychological characterizations which represent a tragicomic blend of human failures and triumphs. The poet's own contemplative reveries, thus oriented, are frequently handled in terms of both implicit and explicit dialogue. For example, in the familiar poem entitled "Mending Wall," the brief narrative represents two opposed attitudes toward tradition, in that the poet imaginatively challenges the literal and therefore meaningless rituals, symbolized by repairing a wall at a point where there is no need for a wall. While the opposed views of the two neighbors are presented with playful seriousness as foils, the conclusion resolves the conflict in favor of the poet's view, as he characterizes his neighbor's typical blindness:

> He moves in darkness as it seems to me,
> Not of woods only and the shade of trees.

9

He will not go behind his father's saying,
And he likes having thought of it so well
He says again, "Good fences make good neighbors."

Thus in these dramatic dialogues, another kind of Frostian matrix is provided through his poetic representation of thought, in various forms of inner and outer dialogue, to provide counterbalanced ways of looking at one and the same thing.

Mountain Interval (1916) takes its title from the side-hill New Hampshire farm above the interval or intervale where the Frost family lived, after returning from England in 1915. The poems in this volume combine the two previously separated modes of the inner lyric vision and the outer narrative contemplation, in ways which reveal increasing poetic subtlety and versatility. For example, while all of Frost's lyrics partake of the dramatic, five lyrics are gathered under the title "The Hill Wife" to provide a miniature drama in five moods rather than acts: obliquely, an isolated woman's cumulative sense of fear, loneliness, marital estrangement, is represented as being so completely misunderstood by her husband that he is baffled when she disappears, irrevocably and without warning. Another foreshadowing of a subsequently favorite Frostian mode occurs in a farm fable entitled "The Cow in Apple Time," a genre portrait which (adapting the tradition of Aesop and La Fontaine) implies with mingled amusement and sadness that the wayward creature's self-injurious action personifies one kind of headstrong and ill-considered human rebellion. Still another indication of Frost's increasing versatility is reflected in his handling of the initial poem intitled "The Road Not Taken." The first-person speaker is unself-consciously and ironically permitted to characterize himself as one who habitually wastes energy in regretting any choice made: belatedly but wistfully he sighs over the attractive alternative rejected. (When this poem was teasingly sent without

10

comment to Frost's English friend, the poet Edward Thomas, who provided the initial inspiration for it, Thomas shamefacedly acknowledged it a good portrait of himself, but not of Frost.) This volume also contains the familiar favorite entitled "Birches."

New Hampshire: A Poem with Notes and Grace Notes (1923) constitutes another kind of new departure, for Frost; this time a venture into the humorous, witty, relaxed realm of gentle social satire, particularly aimed at the American glorification of big business, commercialism, materialism. Taking his inspiration from the *Sermones* of Horace, the poet here sings New Hampshire by praising it for having nothing to sell — just "one each of everything as in a showcase" — and thus being a safe retreat or pleasant contrast to the mercenary drift of other regions. The flat and relaxed conversational tone of the blank-verse lines deliberately risks and largely avoids the prosaic.

The "notes and grace notes" which follow the title poem are lyrics and dramatic narratives which serve as oblique commentaries on the initial text, oblique in that no attempt is made at explicit correlation. The more compressed, terse, clipped lines of the lyrics are strikingly contrasted with the mode of the title poem. Some of the memorable lyrics in *New Hampshire* include "Fire and Ice," "Stopping by Woods," "Dust of Snow," "To Earthward," and "The Need of Being Versed in Country Things."

Of the dramatic narratives and dialogues in this volume, perhaps Frost's most successful one is "The Witch of Coös" (the Biblical place-name is also the name of the northernmost county in New Hampshire). This narrative takes the form of a little drama, beginning with comic overtones and ending with decidedly tragic implications. It begins as an outrageously impossible ghost-story, told collaboratively to the stranger-narrator of the poem by an isolated back-country widow and her grown son; but it accumulates their accidental hints that perhaps their fiction has been used by them for years to let them talk symbolically about a gruesome crime they have otherwise concealed. Psychologically, one gathers, they need to relieve a gnawing sense of guilt by means of the fiction. When the mother concludes her story, she reveals that the intolerable burden of concealment has gradually driven her to the verge of insanity, and she now sees no reason why she ever made a secret of the truth — the "bones" of the "ghost" were those of her former lover:

> "They were a man's his father killed for me.
> I mean a man he killed instead of me."

None of Frost's dramatic psychological characterizations goes more deeply or more subtly into the tragedy of self-betrayal than "The Witch of Coös."

West-running Brook (1928) is particularly important because of the title poem which has already been mentioned and which will be considered in more detail, later. Some of Frost's best lyrics are also contained in this volume, as for example, "Spring Pools," "A Peck of Gold," "Once by the Pacific," "Tree at My Window," "Acquainted with the Night," and "The Soldier."

A Further Range (1936), *A Witness Tree* (1942), and *Steeple Bush* (1947), while adding some excellent lyrics, are volumes too heavily padded with relatively unimpressive and inartistic "editorials" which provide some pointed satirical thrusts at the American scene without adding much to Frost's poetic stature.

Two complementary volumes of verse drama, *A Masque of Reason* (1945) and *A Masque of Mercy* (1947), were eventually and significantly placed together at the end of the collected works which Frost chose to call *Complete Poems* (1949). These two masques will also be considered later, in relation to each other.

Now that we have completed a superficial survey of Robert Frost's separate volumes, in order to gain a comprehensive view, we can come to grips with problems of interpretation which might be phrased in questions such as these: What gains in our understanding of Frost's idiom can be achieved by noticing how some of Frost's dominant and recurrent poetic themes run counter to each other? What essential elements of Frost's poetic theory can be deduced from his poetic practice?

One way to start finding answers to such questions might be taken by remembering that, even though Frost is extremely gifted in his ability to make even the least lyric poem dramatic, he is primarily a subjective lyric poet, at his best in his apparently contradictory moods of response to experience and in his figurative ways of defining differences. As already noticed, the matrix-pattern of *A Boy's Will* foreshadows his persistent pleasure in employing the lyric mode as an expression of self-discovery, even of psychological self-education, concerning his own ties to his beloved, to strangers, to nature, to the universe, to God. If it might be argued that these are the familiar concerns of most lyric poets, one differentiation may be suggested. For Frost, the ultimate and ulterior preoccupation is with a poetic view of life which he can consider complete, in the sense that it encompasses and integrates all these relationships figuratively, and yet not systematically.

His awareness of his differences from conventional attitudes, in his defense of the unsystematic, is at least implied in such a confession as this:

> And were an epitaph to be my story
> I'd have a short one ready for my own.
> I would have written of me on my stone:
> I had a lover's quarrel with the world.

Once again, the contraries implicit in that phrase, "lover's quarrel," do not imply either physical or metaphysical rebellion against the human condition. His poem entitled "Not Quite

Social" contains assurance on that point, an assurance expressed as though he were fearful of being misunderstood:

> You may taunt me with not being able to flee the earth.
> You have me there, but loosely as I would be held.
> The way of understanding is partly mirth.
> I would not be taken as ever having rebelled.

His "lover's quarrel with the world" may have begun through his wanting and trying to discover or define his own sense of simultaneous separateness and integration. More than that, a large part of his poetic pleasure would seem to be derived from his finding verse not only an end in itself but also a means to the end of making each poem some kind of "clarification of life," even a clarification of his own attitude toward life. Presumably there was a time in his youth when he felt relatively comfortable within the framework of inherited and conventional assumptions or beliefs. Yet his poem entitled "The Door in the Dark" develops, with characteristically amusing seriousness, a crucial experience of disillusionment:

> In going from room to room in the dark,
> I reached out blindly to save my face,
> But neglected, however lightly, to lace
> My fingers and close my arms in an arc.
> A slim door got in past my guard,
> And hit me a blow in the head so hard
> I had my native simile jarred.
> So people and things don't pair any more
> With what they used to pair with before.

That figurative dramatization of disillusionment may serve as a reminder that such a plight always heightens the sense of discrepancy between two contrasting ways of looking at anything. Repeatedly, in Frost's lyrics, the playful seriousness evokes ironies and ambiguities which imply that some of the poet's representations of his outward quarrels with the world may also be taken as either conscious or unconscious projections of inward conflicts. At times, some of his poems achieve an extra dimension of meaning if viewed as constructed around his conscious and yet unstated realization of his own divided awareness. His taunts and counter-taunts thus pick up enrichments of meaning if the poet is viewed as contending, at one and the same time, with enemies inside and outside his own heart and mind. Take, for example, Frost's sonnet-like poem (irregular and unrhymed) entitled "For Once, Then, Something." At first glance, the central image of an action represents only the familiar rural pastime of trying to look down through the water, in a well, to see to the bottom, or to see how deep the well is. Yet the metaphorical undertones and overtones are cunningly interwoven:

> Others taunt me with having knelt at well-curbs
> Always wrong to the light, so never seeing
> Deeper down in the well than where the water
> Gives me back in a shining surface picture
> Me myself in the summer heaven godlike
> Looking out of a wreath of fern and cloud puffs.
> *Once,* when trying with chin against a well-curb,
> I discerned, as I thought, beyond the picture,
> Through the picture, a something white, uncertain,
> Something more of the depths — and then I lost it.
> Water came to rebuke the too clear water.
> One drop fell from a fern, and lo, a ripple
> Shook whatever it was lay there at bottom,
> Blurred it, blotted it out. What was that whiteness?
> Truth? A pebble of quartz? For once, then, something.

Such a tantalizing poem may serve to remind us that the ultimate mysteries always provide Frost with his favorite topic for serious play. Although the reader is being gently teased by this ingeniously "metaphysical" development of images, the overt appearance of the question "Truth?" at the beginning of the last line points up the metaphorical preoccupation, here, in terms of

15

two opposed ways of searching for truth. It may even recall an echo of that aphorism attributed to Democritus: "Of truth we know nothing, for truth lies at the bottom of a well." With Frost, as with Democritus, the immediate emphasis is obviously on ultimate truth. But the figurative overtones of the opening lines imply that the speaker has previously acknowledged to "others" (perhaps even to himself) his own limitations of perception, in regard to ultimate truth. That acknowledgment seems to have evoked a taunting kind of criticism. More than that, the choice of words, at the very start of the poem, figuratively identifies ultimate truth with a form of worship: the speaker has been taunted because he "knelt" — "always wrong to the light . . ." It would seem that his faultfinders (again perhaps inner and outer) have claimed that, Narcissus-like, his own failure of vision has caused him to let his own image get between him and the ulterior object of his quest, so that he can "see" only "Me myself in the summer heaven godlike . . ." This complaint apparently provides the taunters with self-justification. But, as this inverted sonnet pattern reaches the conclusion of the single sentence which constitutes the sestet, the speaker moves on into the octave to defend himself with a quiet kind of counter-taunt: perhaps the fault of his failure has not been entirely his own, else how explain the implicitly mysterious rebuke which interrupted his figuratively epistemological search?

If the poem is taken in that sense, the entire tone reflects the poet's rather sly and teasing pleasure in establishing an implied antithesis between the smug certainties of some orthodox views and the tentativeness of the poet's own ambiguous viewpoint, which includes his almost boastfully heretical and unorthodox tendency to approach truth by cautiously accepting and accentuating the limitations of human knowledge. Yet at precisely such a moment the reader should postpone conclusions in order to make room for subsequent modifications which occur within the Frostian manipulations of contraries.

If one is hot on the trail of evidence concerning Frost's heretical views, of course even some of his brief epigrams will tentatively serve:

> They say the truth will make you free.
> My truth will bind you slave to me.

Here again the serious play of wit involves antithetically opposed points of view. The initial assertion directly quotes from the familiar words of Jesus in John 8:32. But the covering assertion implicitly inverts the meaning of those familiar words by suggesting that the acceptance of any so-called ultimate "truth" can be viewed as a limiting action and therefore as a form of enslavement. It would seem that, for Frost, the ultimate truth does indeed lie at the bottom of a very deep well; that he refuses to find that kind of truth subsumed within the dogma of Christian belief.

A remark pertinent here was plaintively made by T. S. Eliot while lecturing at the University of Virginia in 1933: ". . . the chief clue to the understanding of most contemporary Anglo-Saxon literature is to be found in the decay of Protestantism. . . . I mean that amongst writers the rejection of Christianity — Protestant Christianity — is the rule rather than the exception . . ." That postulate is provocative and helpful for anyone trying to understand Frost's chronic tendency to tease the orthodox Christian believer; but again no quick conclusions can be reached. Eliot's remark may further remind us of the often noticed fact that Protestantism has unintentionally encouraged the individual seeker to formulate his own beliefs quite apart from any established sect or creed. In America, the Puritan nonconformists who had fled from Archbishop Laud to indulge their own rigorous beliefs very soon discovered other kinds of nonconformity de-

17

veloping to plague them, even in their midst. Frost, who boasts
of his Puritan descent, and who is decidedly puritanical in many
of his sympathies, might be viewed as a nonconforming Puritan
nonconformist.

For the sake of poetry, there would seem to be a kind of con-
venience or luxury or at least artistic usefulness in the very
posture of heresy. It provides the artist not only with greater
freedom to manipulate his raw materials but also with the added
chance to indulge varying moods of belief and unbelief. He can
say with Horatio, "So I have heard and do in part believe." But
in Frost's case it would seem more accurate to suggest that his
poetic flaunting of heresies largely stems from his inability to
derive adequate intellectual-emotional-spiritual satisfaction from
any systematic dogma which imposes intolerable limitations on
a temperament which delights to seek truth through questions
and dialogue.

Before considering Frost's thematic affirmations, we may profit-
ably stay with his doubts and negations a bit longer. For various
and complicated reasons, his fluctuating and ambiguous viewpoint at times indulges moods which discourage any too-comfort-
ing or too-optimistic sense of benevolent design in nature. One of
his sonnets which has occasionally been singled out for particular
praise is a dark study-in-white, ambiguously entitled "Design":

> I found a dimpled spider, fat and white,
> On a white heal-all, holding up a moth
> Like a white piece of rigid satin cloth —
> Assorted characters of death and blight
> Mixed ready to begin the morning right,
> Like the ingredients of a witches' broth —
> A snow-drop spider, a flower like froth,
> And dead wings carried like a paper kite.
>
> What had that flower to do with being white,
> The wayside blue and innocent heal-all?

What brought the kindred spider to that height,
Then steered the white moth thither in the night?
What but design of darkness to appall? —
If design govern in a thing so small.

Taken out of context, that sonnet might seem to carry overtones more ominous than the context of Frost's other poems
actually permits. By contrast, if this sonnet is considered in relation to the other poems, it suggests not so much a mood of
depressed brooding over "the design of darkness to appall" but
rather a grim pleasure in using such a peculiar *exemplum* for
challenging and upsetting the smug assurance of complacent
orthodox belief concerning Who steers what where, and how. Yet
this sonnet resists even that much reduction. For Frost, the
attempt to see clearly, and from all sides, requires a willingness
to confront the frightening and the appalling in even its darkest
forms.

Any careful reader of Frost's poems notices how frequently
"fear" provides different kinds of premises for him. If nature and
human nature have the power to reduce man to a fearful sense
of his own smallness, his own lostness, in a seemingly indifferent
or even malicious universe, then one suggested way to confront
such fear is to imagine life stripped down to its most naked
forms in order to decide what is left to go on with, and to weigh
the question as to whether the possible gains are worth the neces-
sary cost. As already hinted, the structural pattern of moods in
A Boy's Will may be viewed in this light. But many of the later
poems even more closely represent the confrontations of fear,
lostness, alienation, not so much for purposes of shuddering as for
purposes of overcoming fright, first through individual and then
through social ingenuity, courage, daring, and action.

Several years ago, when Frost was asked to name some of his

favorite books, he mentioned Defoe's *Robinson Crusoe* and Thoreau's *Walden* as thematically rhyming for him: *"Robinson Crusoe* is never quite out of my mind. I never tire of being shown how the limited can make snug in the limitless. *Walden* has something of the same fascination. Crusoe was cast away; Thoreau was self-cast away. Both found themselves sufficient. No prose writer has ever been more fortunate in subject than these two." By implication, no subject matter has ever made stronger appeal to Frost, for poetry, than that same question as to how the limited man can make snug in the limitless. As it happens, many of Frost's poems talk back and forth to each other as though calculated to answer something like Pascal's old-new observation, "When I consider the brief span of my life, swallowed up in the eternity before and behind me, the small space that I fill, or even see, engulfed in the infinite immensity of spaces which I know not, and which know not me, I am afraid." Understanding that kind of fear, Frost expresses much the same mood, with a twist, in his poem entitled "Desert Places." But he more often prefers to answer the existential problem of "what to make of a diminished thing" by representing characters who confront the excruciations with various kinds of order-giving action. In his dramatic monologue entitled "An Empty Threat," the speaker is a fur trader who has chosen to work out his purposes almost alone, on the frozen shore of Hudson Bay. Although he recognizes all the symbols of defeat and death in the bleak landscape, the speaker is represented as uttering his flat rejoinder, "I stay," in the first line of the poem. What can a man make of such expansive diminishment? He considers the extremes of contradictory possibility:

> Give a head shake
> Over so much bay
> Thrown away
> In snow and mist

That doesn't exist,
I was going to say,
For God, man or beast's sake,
Yet does perhaps for all three.

The question of plan or design thus obliquely raised suggests answers not so much in terms of the known or unknown but rather in terms of the possible. The poem concludes with the suggestion that if man is given his choice of succumbing to paralyzing doubts and fears, or of translating even limited faith into possibly constructive action, then the choice is quickly made.

An amusing yet serious variant on that same theme occurs in the ambiguous animal fable entitled "A Drumlin Woodchuck," wherein the creature which makes his home in the sandbank left by the ice-age glacier explains to his mate in tones of snug-and-smug pride that he has adequately constructed their home as a defense against at least the foreseeable forms of destruction. Poetically considered, the woodchuck's boast symbolizes a process of asserting creative design which is immediately meaningful, even "though small, as measured against the All." Viewed in that sense, the poet's own creation of order in verse forms takes on a doubly symbolic meaning. Frost has said as much in his highly poetic prose:

"We people are thrust forward out of the suggestions of form in the rolling clouds of nature. In us nature reaches its height of form and through us exceeds itself. When in doubt there is always form for us to go on with. Anyone who has achieved the least form to be sure of it, is lost to the larger excruciations. I think it must stroke faith the right way. The artist, the poet, might be expected to be the more aware of such assurance. But it is really everybody's sanity to feel it and live by it . . . The background is hugeness and confusion shading away from where we stand into black and utter chaos; and against the background any small man-made figure of order and concentration. What pleasanter than that this should be so . . . To me, any little form I assert on it is velvet, as the saying is, and to be considered for how much more it is than nothing. If I were a Platonist I should have to consider it, I suppose, for how much less it is than everything."

There again, not-knowing is balanced off against knowing-at-least-enough, and doing-at-least-enough, to provide different kinds of formal defense against different kinds of chaos. But notice the cautious observation, "I think it must stroke faith the right way." Faith in what? If man finds himself encompassed merely by hugeness and confusion which shades away into black and utter chaos, then faith in self might seem to be inadequate. But if the rolling clouds of nature suggest form, and if nature reaches its height of form in man, then Frost implies that another possibility may exist in some ulterior form-giving Power back of nature, no matter how much is left in doubt. Even though he likes to indulge at least the posture of not-knowing one gradually discovers that not too much would seem to be left in doubt, for him. If there are times when he seems to take particular pleasure in defining his beliefs in terms of his heresies, he cannot play metaphorical hide-and-seek too long without trailing clouds of puritanic certainty. For example, one of his most paradoxical and most metaphysical poems begins by tantalizing the reader with ambiguities, and even continues with various forms of teasing provocation through the last line:

> A head thrusts in as for the view,
> But where it is it thrusts in from
> Or what it is it thrusts into
> By that Cyb'laean avenue,
> And what can of its coming come,
>
> And whither it will be withdrawn,
> And what take hence or leave behind,
> These things the mind has pondered on
> A moment and still asking gone.
> Strange apparition of the mind!

But the impervious geode
Was entered, and its inner crust
Of crystals with a ray cathode
At every point and facet glowed
In answer to the mental thrust.

Eyes seeking the response of eyes
Bring out the stars, bring out the flowers,
Thus concentrating earth and skies
So none need be afraid of size.
All revelation has been ours.

Perhaps Frost has arranged the enigmatic beginning of "All Revelation" to let the reader act out an important aspect of his central meaning. He requires of us a persistent exercise of seeking and of "mental thrust" merely to understand the literal level of poetic statement. Insofar as the poem has a narrative element, it could be said to start *in medias res*, for symbolic purposes. The controlling image is "the impervious geode," that smooth round kind of stone which contains a cavity lined with crystals. Even in the third stanza the reader gains only an oblique awareness of implied "story" which may be rearranged and chronologically summarized as follows. Someone, recognizing the inner possibilities from the outer shape, has found and cut an entrance into a huge geode, then has taken the trouble to illuminate the crystals with indirect electric lighting, presumably for purposes of inviting others to share and enjoy the wonder of it. Others do come, but what do they see or understand? On that note of questioning, the poem begins: "A head thrusts in as for the view . . ." Immediately the poet raises the psychological question as to what mental-emotional-spiritual preparation may or may not have been brought to focus, in that "view," and what rewards may or may not have been taken away. Yet other acts of sight and insight initially made this experience possible for them, acts of the same sort which are always required before any process of human discovery achieves fulfillment.

In the concluding stanza, poetic generalizations extend the significances of response to the symbolic geode, through related and figurative reminders that man has the power, within himself, to overcome various kinds of strangeness in the universe. To that degree, man finds himself relatively sufficient to cope with all he needs to know of the unknown. But the last line may be viewed as ambiguous. "All revelation has been ours" might be taken to suggest that man endows nature with whatever meaning it has. If that reading would be sufficiently attractive to some, it would scarcely be congenial to Frost's larger context of poetic utterances. On reconsideration, we might notice that the one who discovered beneath the plain surface the underlying meaning and wonder of inner crystals did not create either the outer or inner surface. Then by extension, whatever kind of revelation man here makes or achieves, through the uses of sense and skill, implies at least some kind of precedence of order and of design in nature. So the word "revelation" as there poetically operative would seem more meaningful if viewed as a two-way process, or as an act of mysterious collaboration.

Once again, in "All Revelation," the balance of contrary attitudes or points of view, as they involve Frost's recurrent themes, suggests the poet's distaste for lingering too long in moods which merely accentuate the apparent design of darkness to appall, in the structure of the universe; his distaste for stressing too heavily the fright which can be and is derived from too much contemplation of inner and outer desert places. Yet he never lets us forget the limitations. At times, he editorializes or even preaches, poetically, with unabashed and strongly puritanical tones of warning and corrective, against the sin of indulging too much concern for the imponderables, in or beyond nature. In his poem entitled

"Too Anxious for Rivers," the basic arrangement of imagery represents a landscape vista where a stream flowing through the fore-
ground would seem to be blocked off by a mountain in the background. If so, what happens to the river in its attempt to reach
the sea? Taken symbolically or (in this extremely puritanical
poem) taken allegorically, the river is life, the mountain is death,
the sea is the life-beyond-death, and the rebuked questioner implicitly may be any descendant of Adam who has a tendency to
ask too many questions about life and death:

> The truth is the river flows into the canyon
> Of Ceasing to Question What Doesn't Concern Us,
> As sooner or later we have to cease somewhere.
> No place to get lost like too far in the distance.
> It may be a mercy the dark closes round us
> So broodingly soon in every direction.

That regrettable lapse into an allegorical abstraction may seem
to reinforce only Puritan elements of theme. But the poem develops thereafter in such a way as to mock the attempts of both
science and religion to explain first causes and last effects; then
the last stanza blends the ambiguous and the didactic:

> Time was we were molten, time was we were vapor.
> What set us on fire and what set us revolving
> Lucretius the Epicurean might tell us
> 'Twas something we knew all about to begin with
> And needn't have fared into space like his master
> To find 'twas the effort, the essay of love.

The allusion is enough to remind us that, at the beginning of
De Rerum Natura, Venus or love as the great creative force in
nature, is invoked for purposes of attacking and dismissing the
fear of death, the fear of the gods. Lucretius goes on to plead for
an unsystematic enjoyment of life and nature, free from super-
stition. In Frost's poem, this pagan appeal to Lucretius would
seem to constitute a deliberate and calculated displacement or

substitution for Christian notions as to just how love provides divine motivation for the creation and the salvation of man. Further extensions may occur if we recall that life is viewed by Lucretius as a river or stream or flux of everything that runs away to spend itself in death and nothingness except as somehow resisted by the spirit of human beings.

In that sense, "Too Anxious for Rivers" is related to Frost's most revealing poetic statement of continuity: "West-running Brook." There he implicitly invokes images drawn from Lucretius and would seem to blend them with Heraclitan metaphors such as these: the death of the earth gives life to fire, the death of fire gives life to air, the death of air gives life to water, and the death of water gives life to earth, thus figuratively suggesting the endless cycle of birth and death and rebirth and continuity, in nature. In "West-running Brook," Frost further suggests his awareness that Henri Bergson, in his highly poetic theories of "creative evolution," adapts many figures and images from both Lucretius and Heraclitus. Additional kinship between the poetry of Bergson and of Frost may be found in our remembering Bergson's insistence that all dogmas, systems, and logical constructions are so rigid that they interfere with man's direct or intuitive awareness; that the effort of intuition is needed to reverse intellectual straining and to provide a more creative, a more poetic, approach to knowledge.

Frost may have found Bergson's habit of mind even further congenial to his own because of Bergson's Lucretian insistence that life or spirit is a movement which runs counter to the dead flux of matter, "a reality which is making itself in a reality which is unmaking itself." The stream image occurs and recurs, throughout Bergson, together with the image of man's vital and creative and spiritual resistance to the flow of mere matter: "Life as a whole, from the initial impulsion that thrust it into the world,

will appear as a wave which rises, and which is opposed by the
descending movement of matter." If we keep in mind these
images and views of Lucretius, Heraclitus, and Bergson, then
Frost's literal and symbolic and even metaphysical meanings in
"West-running Brook" may be more easily understood. After the
husband and wife have compared thoughts, in dialogue, concerning the symbolism of the black stream, catching on a sunken
rock, and thus flung backward on itself in the white wave, the
husband is permitted to make this interpretation of that symbol:

> "Here we, in our impatience of the steps,
> Get back to the beginning of beginnings,
> The stream of everything that runs away.
> Some say existence like a Pirouot
> And Pirouette, forever in one place,
> Stands still and dances, but it runs away,
> It seriously, sadly, runs away
> To fill the abyss' void with emptiness.
> It flows beside us in this water brook,
> But it flows over us. It flows between us
> To separate us for a panic moment.
> It flows between us, over us, and *with* us.
> And it is time, strength, tone, light, life, and love —
> And even substance lapsing unsubstantial;
> The universal cataract of death
> That spends to nothingness — and unresisted,
> Save by some strange resistance in itself,
> Not just a swerving, but a throwing back,
> As if regret were in it and were sacred.
> It has this throwing backward on itself
> So that the fall of most of it is always
> Raising a little, sending up a little.
> Our life runs down in sending up the clock.
> The brook runs down in sending up our life.
> The sun runs down in sending up the brook.
> And there is something sending up the sun.
> It is this backward motion toward the source,

Against the stream, that most we see ourselves in,
The tribute of the current to the source.
It is from this in nature we are from.
It is most us."

Here we, in our attempt to understand the art and thought of
Robert Frost, would seem to have arrived at a philosophic mood
diametrically opposed to that which we found expressed in the
sonnet entitled "Design." Notice that the evident design which
Frost finds symbolized in that wave image lends itself to the
creative process in human life, thought, art, action: that which
runs counter to itself establishes a closely interlocked continuity
between man and even that in nature which is hostile or indifferent to man. Moreover, that which runs counter establishes a
symbolic relationship of both man and nature to the source.

If Frost seems cautiously hesistant to define the source, one implicit corollary is that the Creator's revelations, through nature,
as viewed by Frost, are equally indirect, emblematic, contradictory, even discontinuous, and highly symbolic. Moreover, while
much of Frost's poetry suggests that he cannot resist figurative
utterances concerning his wavering and yet centered spiritual
preoccupations, we have at least seen that he often prefers to
reveal-conceal some of his most intimate and personal beliefs
through poetic indirections which grow more meaningful because they do contain and maintain elements of self-contradiction.

Yet it can be demonstrated that from his early lyrics in *A Boy's
Will* (such as, for example, "A Prayer in Spring") to his latest
major poem, "Kitty Hawk," Frost's representations of the venture
of spirit into matter are most meaningfully understood if interpreted, even in their most paradoxical passages, as expressions of
worship, even prayer. Frost's central point of departure (or return) is a firmly rooted belief in both nature and human nature
as at least poetically relatable within a design which has its

ultimate source in a divine plan, a plan with which man collaborates to the best of his limited ability.

That recurrent theme of collaboration is perhaps given its most explicit statement at the conclusion of the poem entitled "Two Tramps in Mudtime." The initial action there represents the poet as engaged in the ritualistic routine of splitting firewood in his farmyard, and as enjoying the play of such work until he is embarrassed by the passing presence of two expert lumberjacks. Their mocking comment suggests that they need, and could better perform, precisely that kind of work. The poet is aware that if his own motive is more love than need, and if their motive is more need than love, perhaps he should relinquish the task to them, for pay. Nevertheless, he concludes with puritanical assertiveness, there are other factors to consider:

> But yield who will to their separation,
> My object in living is to unite
> My avocation and my vocation
> As my two eyes make one in sight.
> Only where love and need are one,
> And the work is play for mortal stakes,
> Is the deed ever really done
> For Heaven and the future's sakes.

What has happened, then, to Frost's recurrent elements of theme involving fear, isolation, lostness, not-knowing, and discontinuity? They remain operative in the poems, side by side with these recurrent elements of faith and love and continuity. His juxtaposition of contrary and yet ultimately complementary images and themes finds its most elaborately paradoxical expression in those two masques which Frost chose to place in a significant summary position, at the conclusion to his volume which he also chose to entitle, with figurative overtones, *Complete Poems*.

As the titles suggest, *A Masque of Reason* and *A Masque of Mercy* explore contrary themes; yet once again they are contraries

29

which permit us to view the two masques as complementary. More than that, they provide an epitome, or a gathering metaphor, of many major themes developed by Frost in the poems which precede and succeed them. Relationships are again explored in each of the masques; man's ultimate relationships to self, to society, to nature, to the universe, to God. Or, to say it another way, the two masques further extend themes involving man's perennial sense of isolation and communion, of fear and courage, of ignorance and knowledge, of discontinuity and continuity.

In *A Masque of Reason*, Frost anticipated what Archibald MacLeish has more recently and more artistically done in building a modern philosophical drama out of the Biblical story of Job for purposes of exploring possible meanings within and behind man's agony. The answers offered by MacLeish, in *J.B.*, primarily emphasize humanistic values, in that the conclusion of the action finds human love the best justification and the best defense. By contrast, the answers offered by Frost are attempts to justify the ways of God to men, thus making Frost's emphasis ultimately metaphysical and theistic. Significantly, earth provides the setting for MacLeish's drama, while heaven provides an ambiguous setting for Frost's masque.

In the initial action, Frost represents Job, his wife, and God as conducting an intimate post-mortem concerning the strengths and weaknesses of human reason in trying to understand the divine plan or design. Intimacy permits Job to ask his questions with all the ardor, boldness, even insolence of one participating in a family quarrel. If the orthodox reader should find himself offended by such apparent irreverence, or should find God represented in terms contrary to trite conventional concepts, the implicit mockery of accepted notions is again not accidental.

Because the action begins some two thousand years after the

death of Job, all the characters have the advantage of encompass-
ing modern knowledge and attitudes, so that the seeming anach-
ronisms of reference suggest continuity in time and space. Job's
concern is to ask God's "reason" for inflicting torture on innocent
human beings. After preliminary hesitancy and sparring, God
takes occasion to thank Job for his collaboration in an epoch-
making action:

> I've had you on my mind a thousand years
> To thank you someday for the way you helped me
> Establish once for all the principle
> There's no connection man can reason out
> Between his just deserts and what he gets.

That phrase, "the way you helped me," may recall notions
advanced by William James and others concerning a suffering
God, limited and thwarted in his plan to realize his divine purpose so long as man is indifferent and uncooperative. Also echoed
throughout the masque is the related Bergsonian concept of a
continuously creative process which develops the universe. But
as Frost adapts these assumptions to his own sympathetic uses, he
combines them with his favorite puritanic emphasis on the limitations of reason as it affects the relationship between man and
God: "there's no connection man can *reason* out . . ." God is
represented as continuing his explanation to Job:

> Virtues may fail and wickedness succeed.
> 'Twas a great demonstration we put on. . . .
> Too long I've owed you this apology
> For the apparently unmeaning sorrow
> You were afflicted with in those old days.
> But it was of the essence of the trial
> You shouldn't understand it at the time.
> It had to seem unmeaning to have meaning.

The phrase "it was of the essence of the trial" may permit a
further reminder here that Frost's earlier poems can be taken as

notes and grace notes to these two masques. He had previously
honored the conventional puritanic tendency to heap a heavy
burden of meaning on the word "trial." In *A Boy's Will*, the
poem entitled "The Trial by Existence" creates a mythic view of
Heaven to dramatize metaphysical mysteries. The central action
of the poem represents the moment when certain souls among the
angelic hosts daringly choose earthly existence as a form of collaborative trial, even though "the pure fate to which you go / Ad-
mits no memory of choice, / Or the woe were not earthly woe / To
which you give the assenting voice." That early poem concludes
with an equally puritanical notion that "life has for us on the
wrack / Nothing but what we somehow chose," even though we
cannot remember that initial choice. In *A Masque of Reason*,
these various views are again invoked and now mingled with
Jamesian-Bergsonian notions, as God reviews the changing or
evolving attitude of man toward God, achieved with the help of
Job and others. The immediate passage continues:

> And it came out all right. I have no doubt
> You realize by now the part you played
> To stultify the Deuteronomist
> And change the tenor of religious thought.

By implication, the Book of Deuteronomy, containing the laws
of Moses, asserted certain incorrect notions as to the extent of
God's being under obligation to reward all for doing good, and
to punish all for doing ill, notions which implied that if man follows the commandments, he prospers, that if man does not, he
fails. Because Job had helped correct these misunderstandings,
God is wryly grateful to Job:

> My thanks are to you for releasing me
> From moral bondage to the human race.
> The only free will there at first was man's,
> Who could do good or evil as he chose.

I had no choice but I must follow him
With forfeits and rewards he understood —
Unless I liked to suffer loss of worship.
I had to prosper good and punish evil.
You changed all that. You set me free to reign.
You are the Emancipator of your God,
And as such I promote you to a saint.

If viewed in these historical and evolutionary terms, the proph-
ets of the Old Testament might also be considered as related
emancipators because they advanced new concepts of God. Hosea
revealed him as a God of justice, Amos revealed him as a God of
love. ("All revelation has been ours.") Later in the action of the
masque, God is represented as saying to Job, "I'm a great stickler
for the author's name. / By proper names I find I do my think-
ing." By extension, that concept is congenial to Frost's way of
viewing thought as a form of dialogue. Here Job is represented
as having been a prophet, without previously realizing it.

But Job, not yet satisfied with God's explanation of suffering,
says at one point, "Such devilish ingenuity of torture / Did seem
unlike You . . ." God has already admitted to Job that even as
Job had been one of his helpers, so Satan had been another, with
all his originality of sin. Job's wife helps by describing Satan as
"God's best inspiration." In other words, good needs evil to com-
plement it, else each would be meaningless. The conclusion of
the masque represents God as confessing his motive had initially
been that simple: "I was just showing off to the Devil, Job." To
complete the symbolic grouping of collaborators, the Devil is
invited on stage, and Job's wife quickly grasps her camera to take
an emblematic picture of God and Satan, with Job standing pre-
cariously between them.

Considered as a work of art, *A Masque of Reason* is too largely
composed of talk-talk, and too little dependent on action, to give

33

it dramatic merit. But if considered as poetry, it can at least serve
to clarify and unify many of the contrary meanings in the earlier
and later poems. Notice that Frost's mockery of conventional religious concepts is here once again counterbalanced by sympathetic representations of theological views which, however fragmen-
tary, are quite in accord with certain elements of Calvinistic Puritan doctrine. The masque thus provides further evidence that no
matter how much Frost may have thought he rejected the received assumptions of his religious heritage, he has indulged that
posture of rejection, through his art and thought, to realize a
difference which was never too pronounced.

Similarly, in Frost's artistic manipulation of *A Masque of
Mercy,* while the inspiration is provided by the Biblical story of
Jonah as prophet, and while the heretical flavor or tone of the
handling is quite obvious, the action eventually resolves into
notions congenial to a fairly conventional viewpoint. The setting,
this time, is a small bookstore in New York City. The action begins just at closing time, when a conversation between the owner
of the bookstore (named Keeper) and his wife (named Jesse Bel)
and a lingering friend and customer (named Paul) is interrupted
by the frenzied entrance of a Jonah-possessed fugitive who an-
nounces fearfully, "God's after me!" (and a moment later) "[To]
make me prophesy . . . This is the seventh time I have been
sent/To prophesy against the city evil." The other characters
quickly discover his motivation for flight:

> I've lost my faith in God to carry out
> The threats He makes against the city evil.
> I can't trust God to be unmerciful.

The customer, Paul, takes charge and assures the fugitive Jonah
that he is a self-deceived escapist,

> . . . though you are not
> Running away from Him you think you are

> But from His mercy-justice contradiction.
> . . . I'm going to make you see
> How relatively little justice matters.

Thus the central theme of the masque becomes overtly established, and is elaborated through a dramatic clash of the four opposed points of view, expressed largely in dialogue, not in action. The basic resolution involves the gradual surrender of certain Old Testament attitudes toward the primacy of justice, in favor of the New Testament emphasis on the primacy of mercy. Eventually Jonah is led to confess, "I think I may have got God wrong entirely. . . Mercy on me for having thought I knew." Jesse Bel, true to her Biblical name, assumes the posture of a modern false-prophetess who would corrupt mankind into immorality and idolatry, and who is thus beyond redemption. Keeper, motivated by socialistic concerns for his brother man, as his name suggests, initially ridicules the attitudes of the other three characters; then gradually he discovers and expresses a sympathetic agreement with the Pauline attitude.

Taken in a slightly different sense, the dominant thematic concern of *A Masque of Mercy* may be said to pivot once again on the limitations of human knowledge as it involves different responses to different kinds of fear, starting and ending with the wisdom-unwisdom of man's fearing God. Indirectly, these notions are related to the convictions of Job, in the earlier masque, that no matter what "progress" may be, it cannot mean that the earth has become an easier place for man to save his soul; that unless earth can serve as a difficult trial-ground, the hardships of existence become meaningless.

Here once again, in the attitudes of both Jonah and Paul, the puritanical views dominate. At one moment Paul is permitted to fall back on Book Three of *Paradise Lost* to make his meaning clear:

35

> . . . After doing Justice justice,
> Milton's pentameters go on to say,
> But Mercy first and last shall brightest shine,
> Not only last, but first, you will observe.

As the fugitive Jonah begins to understand Paul, he in turn is permitted to make his own adjustment to Paul's brand of puritanism by invoking a celebrated passage in *Pilgrim's Progress:*

> You ask if I see yonder shining gate,
> And I reply I almost think I do . . .

But in the denouement of the action, fear again provides the center of attention. Paul concludes by answering Keeper's remarks about the fear of death and judgment, thus:

> We have to stay afraid deep in our souls
> Our sacrifice, the best we have to offer,
> And not our worst nor second best, our best,
> Our very best, our lives laid down like Jonah's,
> Our lives laid down in war and peace, may not
> Be found acceptable in Heaven's sight.
> And that they may be is the only prayer
> Worth praying. May my sacrifice
> Be found acceptable in Heaven's sight.

Paul is closely paraphrasing a familiar passage in Psalm 19:14: "Let the words of my mouth, and the meditations of my heart, be acceptable in thy sight, O Lord, my strength and my redeemer." This prayer and this preachment, so central to the recurrent didacticism and puritanism throughout Frost's poems, reinforce the significance of his emphasis on settling for limited knowledge, provided sufficient courage and resourcefulness can be mustered for translating man's predicament into an act of collaboration. In *A Masque of Reason*, Job was permitted to set up and then to attack an opposed view of life in these lines:

> We don't know where we are, or who we are.
> We don't know one another; don't know You;

Don't know what time it is. We don't know, don't we?
Who says we don't? Who got up these misgivings?
Oh, we know well enough to go ahead with.
I mean we seem to know enough to act on.

So we return to where we started in considering the positive affirmations within Frost's poems: action, in the living present, is recurrently represented as providing different forms of human redemption, atonement, salvation, if only such action is viewed as collaborative with whatever little man can understand of the divine design.

Robert Frost has never chosen to summarize more than fragments of his poetic theory, and yet certain essentials of it can be deduced from his poetic practice. If we remember that his wide acclaim has been earned during an era of artistic innovation and experiment, we may marvel at his having achieved such distinction merely by letting his idiom discover old ways to be new, within the traditional conventions of lyric and dramatic and thematic modes. While Yeats, Eliot, Pound, and others invoked or invented elaborate mythic frames of reference which have enriched and complicated artistic strategies, Frost would seem to have risked successfully the purification of poetic utterance, in complicating simple forms. As we have seen, however, he quite consciously assimilates to his own New England idiom such varieties of classical conventions as the relaxed modes of the Theocritan idylls, the terse epigrammatic brevity of Martial, the contemplative serenity of Horace, the sharply satirical intensity of Juvenal, the homely didacticism of Aesop. Yet his treasured firsthand familiarity with and admiration for the classics have not been displayed in ways which make his meanings depend on esoteric scholarship. Quite clearly, he has deliberately chosen to address himself to the common reader.

But if the majority of Frost's admirers would seem content to share the poet's delight in cherishing the humble beauties of nature, recorded by him with such precision of response to images of experience among New England fields, farms, roadsides, and forests, those readers have been willing to settle for too little, when so many other and deeper levels of meaning are available in his poems. It has frequently and correctly been pointed out that Frost's poetic concerns are akin to those which led Wordsworth to choose incidents and situations from common life and then to present them in a language actually used by the common man whose heartfelt passions are not restrained. Like Wordsworth, and like many poets before and after Wordsworth, Frost has particularly emphasized his concern for catching within the lines of his poems the rhythms and cadences and tones of human speech. Among modern poets, he has been one of the many who have advocated a capturing of what he has repeatedly referred to as "the sound of sense" or "sound posturing" to provide a complicating enrichment of the underlying metrical rhythm.

Perhaps without his realizing it, Frost's own Puritan heritage has made him find congenial the related theories of Coleridge, Wordsworth, and Emerson, particularly in matters related to the organic growth of a poem and the organic relationship between imagery and symbol. "When I see birches bend to left and right," says Frost, "I like to *think* . . ." There it is. His primary artistic achievement, which is an enviable one, in spite of shortcomings, rests on his blending of thought and emotion and symbolic imagery within the confines of the lyric. It would seem to be an essential part of both his theory and practice to start with a single image, or to start with an image of an action, and then to endow either or both with a figurativeness of meaning, which is not fully understood by the reader until the extensions of meaning are found to transcend the physical.

38

Robert Frost

While no one could correctly call Frost a Transcendentalist, his kinship with Emerson goes deeper than might at first be noticed. One approach to this relationship, as it involves a basic element of both poetic theory and practice, may be found through Frost's early sonnet entitled "Mowing":

> There was never a sound beside the wood but one,
> And that was my long scythe whispering to the ground.
> What was it it whispered? I knew not well myself;
> Perhaps it was something about the heat of the sun,
> Something, perhaps, about the lack of sound —
> And that was why it whispered and did not speak.
> It was no dream of the gift of idle hours,
> Or easy gold at the hand of fay or elf:
> Anything more than the truth would have seemed too weak
> To the earnest love that laid the swale in rows,
> Not without feeble-pointed spikes of flowers
> (Pale orchises), and scared a bright green snake.
> The fact is the sweetest dream that labor knows.
> My long scythe whispered and left the hay to make.

The initial effect of that sonnet is one of mood, in which the reverie of the worker picks up for contemplation the tactile and visual and audial images in terms of action and of cherishing. The sensuous response is heightened and enriched not only by the speaking tones and modulations and rhythms struck across the underlying metrical pattern of iambics but also by the intricate and irregular sonnet rhyme scheme: a-b-c-a-b-d-e-c d-f-e-g-f-g. Although the mood of the reverie is not interrupted by the somewhat paradoxical generalization in the thirteenth line, the reader is likely to return to that line, puzzling over it and feeling slightly teased by the possible ambiguities. If the fact-as-dream is interpreted as indicating that the entire reverie reflects an intensely sensuous joy in the immediate human experience, that such pleasurable experience constitutes an end in itself, the poem obviously makes sense in those terms. Taken thus, the sonnet clearly is related to that fundamental theme of love and cherishing which runs throughout Frost's poetry. Any other meaning found ought not to displace or cancel that. But if the fact-as-dream might also be interpreted to represent the act of mowing as a means to an end as well as an end in itself, it could serve to symbolize not only a process of being but also a process of becoming, within the farmer-poet's life. The grass is cut and the hay is left to make, for an ulterior purpose.

The context of other poems within which "Mowing" occurs invites and encourages deeper reading. We have noticed that in Frost's poetic theory and practice he likes to endow images and actions with implicitly metaphorical and symbolic meanings until they repeatedly suggest a continuity between his vision of the human "fact" and the divine "fact." We have also noticed that he likes the tension between two ways of looking at such thought-felt moods; that his own moments of doubt, in these matters, seem to afford him the luxury of reaffirmation. In such a context, a poem like "mowing" reveals further kinships between Frost and Emerson. In his essay on "The Poet" Emerson writes, "I find that the fascination resides in the symbol." Frost would agree. Emerson goes on to say that the response of the farmer to nature is a sympathetic form of worship: "No imitation or playing of these things would content him; he loves the earnest of the north wind, of rain, of stone and wood and iron. A beauty not explicable is dearer than a beauty which we can see to the end of. It is nature the symbol, nature certifying the supernatural, body overflowered by life which he worships with coarse but sincere rites." Again Frost would agree, at least in part; but it must be pointed out that Frost's view of nature-as-symbol does not coincide with the Emersonian view. Neither does it coincide with the New England puritanical view of nature-as-symbol. Nevertheless, to those Puritan forefathers against whom both Emerson and Frost partially rebelled, self-reliance was God-reliance. Even those Puritan fore-fathers also insisted that *laborare est orare*. Whatever the differences in the three positions, the likenesses are significant.

"Prayer," says Emerson, with almost puritanical exultation, "is the contemplation of the facts of life from the highest point of view. It is the soliloquy of a beholding and jubilant soul." Frost would be embarrassed to speak out that frankly in open meeting; but his poems obliquely imply his own assent to the notion. The core of his poetic theory, as of his poetic practice, is to be found in his uses of the sensuous responses of loving and cherishing, first as important poetic images of human actions; then, simultaneously, as even more important symbols of divine worship and even of prayer: "May my sacrifice be found acceptable in Heaven's sight."

In conclusion it should be said that the approach here used, in an attempt to increase our appreciation and understanding of Robert Frost's life and art, is only one of many possible approaches. It is calculated to suggest that many elements run counter to themselves, therein, without any ultimate contradictions. It also provides a means of noticing that Frost's entire work is deeply rooted in the American, even in the most vital Puritan, idiom. It is "native to the grain," and yet thoroughly original. No wonder, then, that Robert Frost has earned a place of distinction, at home and abroad, as a major American poet.

⫰ Selected Bibliography

Separate Works of Robert Frost

A Boy's Will. London: David Nutt, 1913; New York: Henry Holt, 1915.
North of Boston. London: David Nutt, 1914; New York: Henry Holt, 1914.
Mountain Interval. New York: Henry Holt, 1916.
New Hampshire: A Poem with Notes and Grace Notes. New York: Henry Holt, 1923.
West-running Brook. New York: Henry Holt, 1928.
A Further Range. New York: Henry Holt, 1936.
A Witness Tree. New York: Henry Holt, 1942.
A Masque of Reason. New York: Henry Holt, 1945.
Steeple Bush. New York: Henry Holt, 1947.
A Masque of Mercy. New York: Henry Holt, 1947.

Selected and Collected Editions

The editions selected for description below are of particular importance because they represent Robert Frost's own winnowings and arrangements.

Selected Poems. New York: Henry Holt, 1923. (Contains 43 poems. Revised in 1928; contains 57 poems. Again revised in 1934; contains 73 poems. An English edition of *Selected Poems* (London: Jonathan Cape, 1936) contains 62 poems chosen and significantly rearranged by the author; this edition also contains introductory essays by W. H. Auden, C. Day Lewis, Paul Engle, and Edwin Muir.)
Collected Poems. New York: Henry Holt, 1930. (Contains 163 poems. Reissued in 1939, with Frost's prose preface entitled "The Figure a Poem Makes.")
Complete Poems. New York: Henry Holt, 1949. (Contains 304 poems and "The Figure a Poem Makes.")
Selected Poems. London: Penguin Books, 1955. (In the Penguin Poets series. Contains 186 poems and a preface by C. Day Lewis.)

Current American Reprints

The Pocket Book of Robert Frost's Poems, edited by Louis Untermeyer. New York: Pocket Books. $.35.
The Poems of Robert Frost. New York: Modern Library (Random House).

42

$1.65. (Contains 207 poems and Frost's introductory essay entitled "The Constant Symbol.")

Bibliography

Clymer, W. B., and Charles R. Green. *Robert Frost: A Bibliography*. Amherst, Mass.: The Jones Library, 1937.

Critical and Biographical Studies

Cook, Reginald L. *The Dimensions of Robert Frost*. New York: Rinehart, 1958.

Cox, Sidney. *A Swinger of Birches: A Portrait of Robert Frost*. New York: New York University Press, 1957.

Munson, Gorham B. *Robert Frost: A Study in Sensibility and Good Sense*. New York: Doran, 1927.

Thompson, Lawrance. *Fire and Ice: The Art and Thought of Robert Frost*. New York: Henry Holt, 1942.